Much Loved Mec

Casseroles Coc

Budget-Friendly and Comforting One Pot Recipes Anyone Can Make

by **Alissa Noel Grey**

Text copyright(c)2025 Alissa Noel Grey

All rights reserved. No part of this publication may be reproduced, distributed, or transmitted in any form or by any means, including photocopying, recording, or other electronic or mechanical methods, without the prior written permission of the publisher, except in the case of brief quotations embodied in critical reviews and certain other noncommercial uses permitted by copyright law

Although every precaution has been taken to verify the accuracy of the information contained herein, the author and publisher assume no responsibility for any errors or omissions. No liability is assumed for damages that may result from the use of information contained within.

Table Of Contents

Mediterranean Comfort Food Made Easy	4
Greek Chicken Casserole	8
Chicken and Chickpea Casserole	9
Chicken and Onion Casserole	10
Chicken Drumstick Casserole	11
Blue Cheese and Mushroom Chicken	12
Chicken and Cauliflower Casserole	13
Chicken and Spinach Casserole with Feta	14
Lemon Garlic Chicken Casserole	15
Chicken and Artichoke Casserole	16
Feta Chicken with Zucchinis	17
Chicken and Tomato Olive Casserole	18
Lamb Casserole with Olives and Lemon	19
Ground Beef and Cabbage Casserole	21
Ground Beef and Lentil Casserole	22
Citrus Pork with Orzo	24
Spicy Pork with Leeks and Orzo	25
Greek-style Baked Pasta	26
Eggplant With Ground Beef	28
Baked Ground Beef Pasta	30
Baked Pasta with Broccoli, Olives and Pancetta	32
Baked Penne with with Spinach, Feta and Fontina	34
Easy Three-Cheese Pasta with Chicken and Mushrooms	35
Ricotta and Spinach Cannelloni	37
Baked Pasta with Ham, Broccoli and Cheese	39
Three Cheese Lasagna	40
Mediterranean Salmon Casserole	42
Salmon with Broccoli	43
Salmon and Spinach with Feta Cheese	44
Baked Sea bass with Peppers and Lemon	45
Simple Baked Sea Bass	46
Spanish Baked Sardines with Potatoes	47
Cheesy Zucchini and Buckwheat Casserole	48
Creamy Buckwheat Casserole	49
Quick Buckwheat Chilli	50

Eggplant and Chickpea Casserole	52
Spicy Chickpea and Spinach Casserole	53
Chickpea, Leek and Olive Stew	54
Bean and Rice Casserole	55
Italian Eggplant Parmesan	56
Green Pea and Rice Casserole	57
Ratatouille	58
Easy Okra and Tomato Casserole	59
Potato and Zucchini Casserole	60
Cauliflower Casserole	61
Hearty Quinoa and Spinach Breakfast Casserole	62
Baked Shakshuka Casserole	63
Greek Zucchini and Cheese Casserole	64
Spanish Potato Casserole	65
Greek Breakfast Casserole	66
Mediterranean Vegetable Breakfast Casserole	68
Bonus: Delicious Low Fat Soup Recipes Inspired by the Mediterranean Diet	70
Mediterranean Chicken Soup	71
Greek Chicken Soup	72
Fish and Noodle Soup	73
Lamb Soup	74
Creamy Potato Soup	75
Leek, Brown Rice and Potato Soup	76
Fast Mediterranean Chickpea Soup	77
About the Author	

Mediterranean Comfort Food Made Easy

We just love the cozy feeling of sitting down with our family to a home-cooked dinner! But we also live in an age when we are constantly on the move and putting a home-cooked meal on the table on a busy weeknight feels like an impossible endeavor.

In this beautifully curated cookbook, author and home cook Alissa Noel Grey brings together a collection of simple, nourishing casserole recipes inspired by her Mediterranean roots and designed for today's busy families.

In an age when packed schedules and daily demands can make home-cooked meals feel impossible, Alissa offers a refreshing, realistic approach: easy, one-pot meals using affordable, everyday ingredients. With an emphasis on wholesome comfort food, these recipes celebrate the heart of Mediterranean living – cooking and eating with joy, simplicity, and love.

What sets this collection apart is its focus on real food that's both healthy and family-friendly, without requiring advanced skills or exotic ingredients. Alissa's recipes are approachable, even for new cooks, and emphasize the benefits of home cooking – from reducing processed foods to controlling salt, highly processed industrial seed oils, and additives.

Drawing from the traditional kitchens of Greece, Spain, Italy, Turkey, and beyond, Alissa reminds us that the Mediterranean diet isn't a restrictive meal plan, but a lifestyle. It's about eating fresh, colorful vegetables, whole grains, heart-healthy fats, and lean proteins – all prepared simply, and enjoyed with those we love.

Casseroles, the star of this book, are reimagined here as superfood-powered meals that combine convenience with health benefits. With ingredients like chickpeas, lentils, kale, spinach, salmon, and herbs, each recipe is designed to be:

Healthy – rooted in one of the world's most studied and recommended diets

Easy – with straightforward instructions and widely available ingredients

Budget-Friendly – turning simple staples into deeply satisfying meals

Family-Tested – comforting and deliciously tempting for even picky eaters

From quick weeknight dinners to simple make-ahead lunches and breakfasts, these Mediterranean-inspired casseroles are tailored to support a balanced lifestyle – while bringing warmth and flavor to every table.

Alissa also outlines the core principles of the Mediterranean diet, offering readers clear, actionable guidelines to improve heart health, reduce inflammation, boost brain function, and support long-term wellness. By following the Mediterranean way of eating, readers can enjoy:

- **A well-balanced diet of whole, natural foods**
- **Improved cardiovascular and brain health**
- **Reduced risk of chronic illness**
- **Increased energy and sustainable weight management**

Throughout the book, readers are gently encouraged to embrace small, lasting changes – eating more vegetables, using olive oil instead of butter, adding legumes and fish to weekly meals, and enjoying wine and dessert in moderation.

Cooking should never feel overwhelming – and with these superfood-rich Mediterranean casseroles, it won't. With this book, Alissa Noel Grey invites readers to rediscover the joy of simple, home-cooked meals that nourish the body and bring people together.

So grab a baking dish, preheat the oven, and get ready to transform the way you cook – one delicious, wholesome recipe at a time.

The Mediterranean diet will help you:

- Eat a well-balanced diet of whole natural foods
- Prevent heart disease, diabetes, arthritis, Alzheimer's, Parkinson's and cancer
- Lower cholesterol levels and blood pressure
- Improve cardiovascular health
- Improve brain and eye health
- Eat foods that are high in good fats and dietary fiber
- Lose weight
- Increase energy

Just remember these rules to be certain that you are really following a Mediterranean diet:

- Eat vegetables with every meal and eat fresh fruit every day;
- Use olive oil when cooking. Use little or no butter at all;
- Include at least two legume meals per week – add lentils, chickpeas or beans to salads, soups or casseroles.
- Include at least two servings of fish per week: oily fish, if possible, such as salmon, mackerel, gem-fish, canned sardines and canned salmon;

- Eat smaller portions of lean meat – mainly chicken, lamb, and beef;
- Eat yogurt and cheese in moderation;
- Consume wine in moderation, only with meals;
- Eat nuts, seeds, fresh fruit and dried fruit as snacks and dessert;

Greek Chicken Casserole

Serves: 4

Prep time: 45 min

Ingredients:

4 chicken tights

1 small onion, chopped

4-5 potatoes, peeled and cubed

1 large carrot, cut

1 lb green beans, trimmed and chopped

1 cup diced, tomatoes

2 garlic cloves, chopped

1 cup feta cheese, crumbled

3 tbsp extra virgin olive oil

salt and black pepper, to taste

Directions:

Heat oil in a large casserole dish over medium heat. Add in onion and chicken and cook for a minute, stirring. Add in black pepper, carrot and garlic and sauté for another minute.

Add in potatoes and cook for 2 minutes, or until they begin to brown. Stir in beans and tomatoes.

Sprinkle with salt and black pepper

 to taste and top with feta. Cover, and bake for 35-40 minutes, stirring halfway through.

Chicken and Chickpea Casserole

Serves: 4

Prep time: 40 min

Ingredients:

8 chicken drumsticks

2 leeks, trimmed, thinly sliced

1 garlic clove, crushed

1 can chickpeas, drained and rinsed (Note: Opt for BPA-free cans)

3 ripe tomatoes, diced

1 tsp dried rosemary

3 tbsp extra virgin olive oil

cooked couscous, to serve

Directions:

In a casserole, gently heat the oil over medium-high heat. Brown the chicken drumsticks for 1-2 minutes, each side.

Add in leeks and garlic and cook, stirring, for 2 minutes or until soft. Add in the tomatoes, chickpeas, and rosemary.

Cover, and bake for 35-40 minutes, stirring halfway through. Season with salt and pepper and serve with couscous.

Chicken and Onion Casserole

Serves: 4

Prep time: 35 min

Ingredients:

4 chicken breasts

4 large onions, sliced

2 leeks, cut

1 cup black olives, pitted

4 tbsp extra virgin olive oil

1 tsp dried thyme

salt and black pepper, to taste

Directions:

Heat olive oil in a large, deep frying pan over medium-high heat. Brown chicken, turning, for 2-3 minutes each side or until golden. Set aside in a casserole dish.

Cut the onions and leeks and add them on and around the chicken, Add in olives, thyme, salt and black pepper to taste.

Cover with a lid or aluminum foil and bake at 375 F for 35-40 minutes, or until the chicken is cooked through.

Uncover and return to the oven for 5 minutes or until the chicken is crispy.

Chicken Drumstick Casserole

Serves: 4

Prep time: 35 min

Ingredients:

8 chicken drumsticks

1 head broccoli, cut into florets

1 leek, sliced

1 garlic clove, crushed

1 sweet potato, peeled and cubed

1 carrot, cut

1 tsp dried rosemary

4 tbsp olive oil

1 tsp dried oregano

salt and black pepper, to taste

Directions:

Heat the olive oil in a non stick frying pan over medium heat. Add the chicken drumsticks and cook, turning occasionally, for 3-4 minutes, or until sealed.

Transfer the chicken to a casserole dish and add in the vegetables on and around. Sprinkle with salt, black pepper and oregano, and bake in a preheated to 375 F oven until cooked through.

Blue Cheese and Mushroom Chicken

Serves 4

Prep time: 30 min

Ingredients:

4 chicken breast halves

5-6 white button mushrooms, chopped

1/2 cup mushroom soup

1/3 cup crumbled blue cheese

1/2 cup sour cream

salt and black pepper, to taste

1/2 cup parsley, finely cut

Directions:

Heat the oven to 350 F. Spray a casserole with non stick spray. Place all ingredients into it, turn the chicken to coat.

Bake for 30-35 minutes or until chicken juices run clear. Sprinkle with parsley and serve.

Chicken and Cauliflower Casserole

Serves 6

Prep time: 35 min

Ingredients:

1/2 head cauliflower, cut in small florets

2 cups cooked chicken, diced

6-7 spring onions, finely cut

8-9 cherry tomatoes, halved

1/2 tsp dried oregano

1 cup shredded cheddar cheese, divided

1 cup sour cream

2 tbsp extra virgin olive oil

salt and black pepper, to taste

Directions:

Steam cauliflower florets until tender, about 8 minutes.

Heat olive oil in a large skillet and sauté onions for 1-2 minutes. Stir in chicken and oregano and cook for 1 minute, stirring.

Combine cauliflower and chicken mixture together in a casserole. Add in the cherry tomatoes and season with salt and pepper to taste.

Combine sour cream and half the shredded cheddar and stir in the casserole. Sprinkle on top the remaining cheddar.

Cover the casserole with foil or a lid and bake for 25-30 minutes, remove foil and bake until cheese is brown and bubbly.

Chicken and Spinach Casserole with Feta

Serves: 4

Prep time: 35 min

Ingredients:

4 chicken breasts

2 cups spinach leaves

½ cup feta cheese, crumbled

2 tbsp olive oil

1 tsp oregano

salt and black pepper, to taste

Directions:

Brown chicken in olive oil, transfer to casserole dish.

Top with spinach and feta, season with oregano, salt, and black pepper.

Cover and bake at 375F for 35 minutes.

Lemon Garlic Chicken Casserole

Serves: 4

Prep time: 40 min

Ingredients:

4 chicken thighs, skin on

2 lemons, sliced

5 garlic cloves, whole, peeled

1 red bell pepper, sliced

2 tbsp olive oil

1 tsp oregano

salt and black pepper, to taste

Directions:

Heat olive oil in a frying pan. Brown chicken thighs for 2–3 minutes on each side.

Place in casserole dish with lemon slices, garlic, and the bell pepper.

Season with oregano, salt, and black pepper. Cover and bake at 375F for 35 minutes. Uncover and bake 5 minutes more until golden.

Chicken and Artichoke Casserole

Serves: 4

Prep time: 45 min

Ingredients:

4 chicken breasts

1 jar artichoke hearts, drained

1 onion, sliced

2 tbsp olive oil

½ cup sun-dried tomatoes, chopped

1 tsp dried basil

salt and black pepper, to taste

Directions:

In a skillet, brown chicken in olive oil for 2 minutes each side.

Transfer to casserole dish. Add artichokes, onion, sun-dried tomatoes, basil, salt, and black pepper.

Cover and bake at 375F for 40 minutes. Uncover and cook 5 minutes longer.

Feta Chicken with Zucchinis

Serves: 4

Prep time: 45 min

Ingredients:

4 boneless, skinless chicken breasts

2 medium zucchinis, peeled and sliced

1 lemon, thinly sliced

2 tbsp extra virgin olive oil

1/2 cup chopped fresh parsley

salt and black pepper, to taste

1/3 cup crumbled feta cheese

Directions:

Preheat oven to 400F.

Drizzle olive oil in a casserole dish and arrange half of the lemon slices on the bottom. Place the chicken on top and season with salt.

In a bowl, combine zucchini, parsley, remaining olive oil, pepper, and remaining lemon slices.

Spread the mixture around the chicken and sprinkle with feta. Bake for 20 minutes or until chicken is cooked through.

Slice chicken into thirds and serve with the zucchini and lemon mixture.

Chicken and Tomato Olive Casserole

Serves: 4

Prep time: 35 min

Ingredients:

4 chicken thighs

2 cups cherry tomatoes

1 small onion, finely cut

½ cup Kalamata olives

½ cup feta cheese, crumbled

3 tbsp olive oil

1 tsp dried thyme

salt and black pepper, to taste

Directions:

In a skillet, brown chicken in olive oil, then arrange in a casserole dish with onion, cherry tomatoes, and olives.

Sprinkle with thyme, salt, and black pepper. Top with feta, cover, and bake at 375F for 35 minutes.

Lamb Casserole with Olives and Lemon

Serves 4

Prep time: 30-40 min

Ingredients:

3 lb boneless lamb shoulder, cut into 1-inch pieces

4-5 large carrots, thinly sliced

1 onion, chopped

2 garlic cloves, crushed

2 cups green olives, pitted

3 cups water

3 tbsp extra virgin olive oil

1 tbsp lemon zest

1 tbsp paprika

1 tsp cumin

1 tsp ground coriander

1 tsp cinnamon

salt and black pepper, to taste

3 tbsp lemon juice

1 cup cilantro leaves, chopped

1/2 cup fresh mint, finely cut

Directions:

In a large bowl, mix the olive oil, garlic, lemon zest, paprika, coriander, cumin, black pepper, saffron, cinnamon and salt. Add the lamb and toss to coat. Refrigerate for at least 4 hours.

Place the lamb and spices into a casserole. Add the water, carrots and onion and bring to a boil. Cover and bake at 375F until the lamb is tender, about 2 hours.

Stir in the olives and cook for 2-3 minutes. Stir in the mint, cilantro and lemon juice and serve.

Ground Beef and Cabbage Casserole

Serves: 4-5

Prep time: 50 min

Ingredients:

1 lb ground beef

1/2 cabbage, shredded

1/2 onion, chopped

2 leeks, white part only, chopped

1 tomato, diced

1 tbsp paprika

1/2 tsp cumin

½ tsp black pepper

4 tbsp extra virgin olive oil

salt, to taste

Directions:

In a deep saucepan, sauté the onion and leeks in olive oil until tender. Add in the ground beef, tomato, paprika, cumin, salt and black pepper.

Place the shredded cabbage on the bottom of an ovenproof baking dish. Cover with beef mixture. Cover with a lid or aluminum foil and bake at 325 F for 40 minutes.

Ground Beef and Lentil Casserole

Serves: 4-5

Prep time: 30 min

Ingredients:

1 lb ground beef

1 small onion, chopped

2 garlic cloves, crushed

2/3 cup dry green lentils

1 carrot, chopped

2 cups water

2 bay leaves

1 tsp dried oregano

1 tbsp paprika

1/2 tsp salt

1/2 tsp cumin

3 tbsp extra virgin olive oil

black pepper, to taste

Directions:

Heat the olive oil in a skillet over medium-high heat. Add the onion and carrot and sauté for 4-5 minutes. Add in garlic and sauté a minute more. Add the ground beef and cook for 4-5 minutes, stirring, until browned. Add the paprika, cumin, and oregano.

Transfer the beef to a casserole dish, add in the bay leaves, tomatoes, lentils and water.

Cover and bake at 375F for 20 minutes or until the beef is cooked through. Remove the bay leaves and serve.

Citrus Pork with Orzo

Serves 5-6

Prep time: 70 min

Ingredients:

2 lb pork shoulder, cut into 1 inch chunks

1 cup orzo

1 cup orange juice

1 cup water

1 large carrot, chopped

6-7 spring onions, finely cut

1-2 garlic cloves, chopped

1 tsp orange zest

1/2 tsp cumin

3 tbsp extra virgin olive oil

Directions:

Heat the olive oil in a large skillet over medium-high heat. Working in batches, brown the pieces of pork shoulder.

Add in the carrots, garlic, orange zest, cumin, salt and black pepper to taste. Stir, and cook for 1-2 minutes, stirring.

Transfer to a casserole dish, add the orange juice and water, cover and bake at 375F for 40 minutes.

Add in the orzo and spring onions, stir to combine and bake for 15 minutes more.

Spicy Pork with Leeks and Orzo

Serves 5-6

Prep time: 70 min

Ingredients:

2 lb pork shoulder, cut into 1 inch chunks

1 cup orzo

1 lb leeks, cut

1 large carrot, chopped

1 red pepper, cut

4-5 garlic cloves, chopped

1 tbsp paprika

1 tsp hot paprika

3 tbsp extra virgin olive oil

2 tbsp tomato paste, dissolved in 1/3 cup water

1 cup water

Directions:

Heat the olive oil in a skillet over medium-high heat. Working in batches, brown the pieces of pork shoulder.

Add in the carrot, pepper, leeks, garlic, salt, black pepper to taste and paprika. Stir, and add the tomato paste.

Transfer to a casserole, cover and bake for 40 minutes. Add in the water and orzo and bake for 15 minutes more.

Greek-style Baked Pasta

Serves 5

Prep time: 25 min

Ingredients:

12 oz small pasta

1 lb lean ground lamb

3 cups marinara sauce

1 onion, finely cut

2 garlic cloves, chopped

2 tbsp olive oil

2 eggs

1 tsp nutmeg

3 cups fresh ricotta cheese

3/4 cup grated Parmesan cheese

salt and black pepper, to taste

Directions:

Gently sauté the onion in olive oil, for 2-3 minutes over medium heat. Add in the ground lamb and garlic and cook for 10 minutes, or until the meat is cooked through. Stir in the marinara sauce. Season with salt and pepper, to taste.

In a blender, blend 2 cups of the ricotta with the eggs, nutmeg and 1/2 cup of the Parmesan cheese until smooth

Meanwhile, cook the pasta according package instructions. Drain and set aside in an oiled baking dish.

Add the lamb mixture to the pasta and toss to combine. Pour the ricotta mixture on top and sprinkle with the remaining Parmesan cheese. Bake the pasta until the cheese turns golden, 15-20 minutes.

Eggplant With Ground Beef

Serves: 6

Prep time: 45 min

Ingredients:

1 lb ground beef

2 eggplants, peeled and cut into thick rounds

1 tbsp salt

1 onion, chopped

2 garlic cloves, crushed

1/2 tsp ground cinnamon

1/2 tsp ground nutmeg

1/4 tsp ground coriander

1 can tomatoes, undrained, chopped

1/2 cup parsley leaves, finely chopped

2 eggs

3 tbsp coconut milk

4 tbsp extra virgin olive oil

salt and black pepper, to taste

Directions:

Peel and cut the eggplant and place the slices on a plate. Sprinkle with a tablespoon of salt and set aside for 30 minutes, then rinse and pat dry.

Heat olive oil in a deep frying pan over medium-high heat. Fry the eggplant slices in batches for 2-3 minutes each side or until golden. Set aside in a plate.

In the same pan, sauté onion and garlic for 2-3 minutes or until transparent. Add in ground beef and spice, mix well and sauté until it turns light brown. Add in tomatoes and parsley and simmer until the tomato sauce thickens.

Place half the eggplant slices in an ovenproof baking dish. Cover with beef and tomato mixture and top with remaining eggplant.

Whisk two eggs with coconut milk. Pour over the meat and eggplant mixture. Bake for 30 minutes or until golden. Set aside for five minutes and serve.

Baked Ground Beef Pasta

Serves 6

Prep time: 25 min

Ingredients:

12 oz small pasta

1 lb ground beef

2 onions, finely chopped

4 garlic cloves, chopped

3-4 mushrooms, chopped

5-6 gherkins, chopped

1 small tomato, diced

1/2 cup parsley leaves, chopped

1 can mushroom soup

salt and black pepper, to taste

1 cup mozzarella cheese, grated

1 egg, whisked

Directions:

Prepare the pasta according to package directions. Drain and place in an ovenproof baking dish.

Heat olive oil in a large pot and gently sauté the onion until transparent. Add in ground beef, mushrooms, garlic and tomato. Stir and cook on low heat for about 10 minutes. When the meat is almost done, add in the gherkins and parsley.

Toss everything with the pasta. Add in the mushroom soup and stir to combine.

Whisk the egg with mozzarella cheese and spread all over the pasta equally. Bake in a preheated to 350 F oven for 10 minutes or until the cheese turns golden.

Baked Pasta with Broccoli, Olives and Pancetta

Serves 6

Prep time: 25 min

Ingredients:

12 oz small pasta

1 1/2 pounds broccoli, cut into small florets

1 lb cherry tomatoes

one 4 oz slice of pancetta, finely diced

1 cup black olives, pitted and halved

1 onion, finely cut

2 garlic cloves, chopped

9-10 fresh basil leaves, chopped

2 cups fresh ricotta cheese

3/4 cup grated Parmesan cheese

2 tbsp extra virgin olive oil

salt and black pepper, to taste

Directions:

Preheat the oven to 425 F and oil an ovenproof baking dish. Add in the tomatoes, broccoli, garlic and basil. Sprinkle with half the olive oil and season with salt and pepper. Roast for about 20 minutes, until softened.

Prepare the pasta according to package directions and toss with the roasted tomatoes, broccoli and garlic.

Meanwhile, in a large, deep skillet, heat the remaining 1

tablespoon of olive oil. Add in the pancetta and cook over moderately high heat, stirring occasionally, until browned and nearly crisp, about 5 minutes. Stir and add the onion. Cook on low heat, stirring occasionally, until softened, about 5 minutes.

Toss everything in the baking dish. Add in the ricotta and Parmesan cheese and stir to combine.

Bake in a preheated to 350 F oven for 10 minutes or until the cheese turns golden.

Baked Penne with with Spinach, Feta and Fontina

Serves 6

Prep time: 25 min

Ingredients:

1 lb penne

1 10 oz package frozen spinach, thawed

1 cup cherry tomatoes, halved

2 garlic cloves, chopped

9-10 fresh basil leaves, chopped

2 cups crumbled feta cheese

6 oz fontina, grated

3/4 cup grated Parmesan cheese

2 tbsp extra virgin olive oil

1/2 tsp nutmeg

Directions:

Preheat the oven to 350 F and oil a ceramic or glass baking dish.

Prepare the pasta according to package directions and put it in the prepared baking dish. Toss with 1 tablespoon of the oil.

Meanwhile, put the spinach in a food processor and puree with the garlic, feta, half Parmesan cheese, the nutmeg, salt, and pepper. Stir in half the fontina.

Toss everything in the baking dish. Add the cherry tomatoes and stir. Top with the remaining fontina and Parmesan. Bake the pasta until the cheese turns golden, 15-20 minutes.

Easy Three-Cheese Pasta with Chicken and Mushrooms

Serves 6

Prep time: 25 min

Ingredients:

1 lb small pasta

9-10 white button mushrooms, chopped

2 cups cooked chicken, diced

1/2 onion, finely cut

2 garlic cloves, chopped

9-10 fresh basil leaves, chopped

2 cups Ricotta cheese

6 oz fontina, grated

3/4 cup grated Parmesan cheese

3 tbsp extra virgin olive oil

1/2 tsp dried oregano

salt and black pepper, to taste

Directions:

Preheat the oven to 350 F and oil an ovenproof baking dish.

Prepare the pasta according to package directions and put it in the prepared baking dish. Toss with 2 tablespoons of the oil.

Meanwhile, in a large, deep skillet, heat the remaining 1 tablespoon of olive oil. Add in the onion and mushrooms and cook over moderately high heat, stirring occasionally, until softened, about 5 minutes. Add the garlic and chicken. Cook on low heat, stirring occasionally, about 2 minutes. Add the Ricotta cheese and half the Parmesan and fontina. Stir to combine.

Toss everything in the baking dish. Top with the remaining fontina and Parmesan. Bake the pasta until the cheese turns golden, 15-20 minutes.

Ricotta and Spinach Cannelloni

Serves 5

Prep time: 25 min

Ingredients:

1 lb dried cannelloni tubes

1 lb chopped spinach

1 onion, finely cut

1 garlic clove, chopped

1/2 cup green olives, chopped

1 lb mascarpone

1 lb ricotta

1 cup milk

1/4 cup toasted pine nuts

1 tsp nutmeg

1 tsp smoked paprika

3 cups fresh ricotta cheese

1/2 cup grated Parmesan cheese

2 tbsp extra virgin olive oil

salt and black pepper, to taste

Directions:

Gently sauté the onion and garlic in olive oil, for 2-3 minutes over medium heat. Add in the spinach and cook for 3-4 minutes, or until it wilts. Season with salt and pepper to taste and add the paprika, pine nuts and green olives.

Set aside to cool and stir in the ricotta cheese.

In a bowl, whisk the mascarpone with the milk, nutmeg, the Parmesan and some salt. Spread half of this mixture into a large ovenproof dish.

Spoon some of the kale filling in each cannelloni tube using a teaspoon, and place the tubes in the dish, snugly together, on top of the mascarpone mixture.

Pour the other half of the mascarpone mixture over the cannelloni tubes, and sprinkle with Parmesan.

Bake in a preheated to 350 F oven for 30 minutes, or until the top is crisp, the sauce is bubbling and the pasta soft.

Baked Pasta with Ham, Broccoli and Cheese

Serves 6

Prep time: 35 min

Ingredients:

2 cups small pasta

1 cup diced ham

1 onion, finely chopped

4 garlic cloves, chopped

3 white button mushrooms, chopped

1 head broccoli, cut in florets

salt and black pepper, to taste

1 cup mozzarella cheese, grated

1 egg, whisked

Directions:

Prepare pasta according to package directions. Drain and place in an ovenproof casserole.

Heat olive oil in a large skillet and sauté onion until transparent. Add in mushrooms, garlic and broccoli, stir, and cook on medium heat for about 10 minutes, stirring.

Combine broccoli and mushroom mixture with pasta and ham. Season with salt and pepper to taste.

Whisk the egg with mozzarella cheese and spread all over the pasta equally.

Bake in a preheated to 350 F oven for 15 minutes, or until the cheese turns golden.

Three Cheese Lasagna

Serves 5-6

Prep time: 40 min

Ingredients:

3 cups loosely packed kale leaves, chopped

4 cups loosely packed spinach

1 cup fresh basil leaves, torn

1 onion, chopped

1 can tomatoes

2-3 garlic cloves, crushed

1 cup grated Parmesan cheese

1 cup ricotta cheese

2 cup mozzarella cheese, shredded

1 cup cream

1 cup vegetable broth

12 no-cook lasagna noodles

1/2 cup Parmesan cheese

Directions:

In a skillet, sauté onion and garlic for a few minutes. Add in spinach, kale, tomatoes and basil and cook over medium heat for about 5 minutes. Season with salt and pepper and stir in cream.

Spread one-third of the greens mixture over the bottom of a greased 13x9x2-inch baking dish. Top with noodles. Layer mozarella, ricotta and Parmesan cheese.

Repeat layering spinach mixture, cheese and noodles two more times. Top with Parmesan cheese and pour over vegetable broth.

Bake for 20 minutes in a preheated to 350F oven. Set aside for at least 10 minutes before serving.

Mediterranean Salmon Casserole

Serves: 4-5

Prep time: 35 min

Ingredients:

2 boneless salmon fillets

1 tomato, thinly sliced

1 onion, thinly sliced

1 tbsp capers

3 tbsp olive oil

1 tsp dry oregano

3 tbsp Parmesan cheese

salt and black pepper, to taste

Directions:

Preheat oven to 350 F. Place the salmon fillets in a baking dish, sprinkle with oregano, top with onion and tomato slices, drizzle with olive oil, and sprinkle with capers and Parmesan cheese.

Cover the dish with foil and bake for 30 minutes, or until the fish flakes easily.

Salmon with Broccoli

Serves: 4

Prep time: 14 min

Ingredients:

4 salmon fillets, skin on

1 lb fresh broccoli florets

2 tbsp soy sauce

2 tbsp toasted sesame oil

1 tsp chili garlic sauce

1 tbsp brown sugar

1/2 cup spring onions, finely cut, to serve

Directions:

In a large bowl, combine the garlic and soy sauce with the sesame oil and brown sugar. Add in the salmon and broccoli and toss to coat.

Place salmon skin side down in a single layer on a lined baking tray. Add the broccoli florets around.

Bake for 10-12 minutes or until the fish is cooked through and flakes easily with a fork. Top with spring onions and serve.

Salmon and Spinach with Feta Cheese

Serves: 4

Prep time: 15 min

Ingredients:

4 salmon fillets, skin on

1 bag frozen spinach

4-5 green onions, chopped

1 cup crumbled feta cheese

3 tbsp extra virgin olive oil

salt and pepper, to taste

lemon wedges, to serve

Directions:

In a skillet, heat olive oil on medium-high. Cook the spinach and the green onions for 2-3 min, stirring once or twice. Season with salt and pepper to taste and add in the feta cheese. Cook for 1 minute more.

Place salmon skin side down in a single layer on a lined baking tray and bake for 10-12 minutes or until it is cooked through and flakes easily with a fork.

Spoon the spinach mixture onto plates, then top with the salmon and serve with lemon wedges.

Baked Sea bass with Peppers and Lemon

Serves: 4

Prep time: 30 min

Ingredients:

4 sea bass fillets

2 bell peppers, sliced

1 lemon, sliced

3 tbsp olive oil

1 tsp parsley

salt and black pepper, to taste

Directions:

Place sea bass in casserole dish with peppers and lemon slices. Drizzle with olive oil, season with parsley, salt, and black pepper. Bake at 375F for 20-25 minutes until flaky.

Simple Baked Sea Bass

Serves: 4

Prep time: 30 min

Ingredients:

4 sea bass fillets

5 oz fennel, trimmed and sliced

5-6 spring onions, chopped

2 garlic cloves, chopped

10 black olives, pitted and halved

2-3 lemon wedges

1 tbsp capers

2 garlic cloves, finely chopped

½ tsp paprika

½ cup dry white wine

3 tbsp extra virgin olive oil

salt and pepper, to taste

Directions:

In a cup, mix garlic, olive oil, salt, and black pepper.

Arrange the sliced fennel in a shallow ovenproof casserole. Add the green onions and lay the fish on top. Pour over the olive mixture. Scatter the olives, paprika and lemon wedges over the fish, then pour the wine over.

Cover the dish with a lid or foil and bake for 20 minutes, or until the fish flakes easily.

Spanish Baked Sardines with Potatoes

Serves: 4

Prep time: 40 min

Ingredients:

1 lb fresh sardines, cleaned

3 potatoes, peeled and sliced

1 medium onion, sliced

2 tomatoes, sliced

3 tbsp extra virgin olive oil

1 tbsp parsley

salt and black pepper, to taste

Directions:

Layer potatoes, onion, and tomatoes in casserole dish. Arrange sardines on top.

Drizzle with olive oil, sprinkle with parsley, salt, and black pepper. Bake at 375F for 30 minutes.

Cheesy Zucchini and Buckwheat Casserole

Serves: 4-5

Prep time: 20 min

Ingredients:

1 cup buckwheat groats

1 cup vegetable broth

1/2 cup crème fraîche

1 cup crumbled feta cheese

1 onion, finely chopped

3 garlic cloves, chopped

4 zucchinis, peeled and diced

1 cup fresh dill, finely cut

2 tbsp extra virgin olive oil

1/2 cup grated Parmesan cheese

Directions:

Toast the buckwheat in a dry saucepan for about 2 minutes, stirring. Set aside.

In an ovenproof casserole, heat olive oil and gently sauté the onion and garlic for 1-2 minutes.

Add in the diced zucchinis and sauté for 1-2 minutes, stirring. Add the toasted buckwheat, vegetable broth, feta cheese, crème fraîche, finely cut dill and salt to taste. Stir to combine and top with Parmesan cheese.

Bake in a preheated to 350F for 20 minutes or until the cheese is golden.

Creamy Buckwheat Casserole

Serves: 4-5

Prep time: 20 min

Ingredients:

1 cup buckwheat groats

1 cup vegetable broth

1/2 cup crème fraîche

1 small onion, chopped

1 zucchini, peeled and chopped

2 carrots, diced

1 cup frozen peas

2 garlic cloves, minced

4 tbsp extra virgin olive oil

salt and pepper, to taste

1 cup parsley, finely cut

Directions:

Toast the buckwheat in a dry saucepan for about 2 minutes, stirring; set aside.

In an ovenproof dish, heat olive oil and gently sauté the onion and garlic for a minute. Add in the green peas, carrots and zucchini and cook, stirring for 3-4 minutes. Add in vegetable broth, crème fraîche and the toasted buckwheat.

Bake in a preheated to 350F for 20 minutes and serve sprinkled with parsley!

Quick Buckwheat Chilli

Serves: 4-5

Prep time: 20-25 min

Ingredients:

1 cup buckwheat groats

1 ¾ cups vegetable broth

1 large onion, finely cut

3 cloves garlic, chopped

1 green bell pepper, chopped

1 can diced tomatoes

1 can mixed beans, well rinsed and drained

1 tbsp paprika

1 tsp chilli powder

1 tsp ground cumin

2 tbsp extra virgin olive oil

¼ cup chopped fresh coriander, to serve

Directions:

Toast the buckwheat in a dry saucepan for about 2 minutes, stirring, then set aside.

In a an ovenproof casserole dish, heat the oil over medium heat. Add the onion, bell pepper and garlic and sauté until softened, about 3 minutes. Stir in the chilli powder, cumin and paprika and sauté for another minute.

Add the buckwheat and stir to combine well. Stir in the tomatoes, beans and vegetable broth.

Bake in a preheated to 350F for 20 minutes. Serve sprinkled with fresh coriander and serve.

Eggplant and Chickpea Casserole

Serves 4

Prep time: 25 min

Ingredients:

2 medium eggplants, peeled and diced

1 large onion, finely cut

2 garlic cloves, chopped

1 15 oz can chickpeas, drained

1 cup canned tomatoes, undrained, diced

1 cup green olives

1 tbsp paprika

1 tsp cumin

3 tbsp olive oil

salt and pepper, to taste

1 cup Parmesan cheese

1 cup parsley leaves, very finely cut, to serve

Directions:

Heat olive oil in a deep casserole dish and sauté onions and garlic. Add paprika and cumin, stir, and sauté for 2-3 minutes, or until the onions have softened.

Add the eggplant, tomatoes, olives and chickpeas and salt and black pepper to taste.

Top with cheese and bake in a preheated to 350F for 20 minutes. Serve sprinkled with parsley.

Spicy Chickpea and Spinach Casserole

Serves: 4

Prep time: 40 min

Ingredients:

1 onion, chopped

3 garlic cloves, chopped

1 15 oz can chickpeas, drained and rinsed

1 15 oz can tomatoes, diced and undrained

1 1 lb bag baby spinach

a handful of blanched almonds

½ cup vegetable broth

1 tbsp hot chilli paste

½ tsp cumin

salt and pepper, to taste

Directions:

In an ovenproof casserole dish, heat olive oil and gently sauté the onion and garlic for 4-5 minutes, or until tender. Add spices and stir.

Add in chickpeas, tomatoes, almonds and broth. Bake in a preheated to 350F for 10-15 minutes.

Add the chilli paste and spinach and bake for 5 minutes. Remove from heat and season with salt and pepper to taste.

Chickpea, Leek and Olive Stew

Serves: 4-5

Prep time: 20 min

Ingredients:

5 cups sliced leeks

25-30 black olives, pitted and halved

1 15 oz can chickpeas, drained

½ cup water

1 tbsp tomato paste

1 cup grated Parmesan cheese

4 tbsp extra virgin olive oil

salt and black pepper, to taste

Directions:

In a deep baking dish, heat olive oil and sauté the leeks for 2-3 minutes. Add in the chickpeas and olives. Dissolve the tomato paste in half a cup of warm water and add it to the chickpeas.

Season with black pepper and bake in a preheated to 350 F oven for 15-20 minutes.

Sprinkle with Parmesan cheese and bake for 3-4 minutes more.

Bean and Rice Casserole

Serves: 4-5

Prep time: 30 min

Ingredients:

2 15 oz cans white or red beans, drained

1 cup water or vegetable broth

2/3 cup rice

2 onions, chopped

½ bunch parsley, finely cut

7-8 fresh mint leaves, finely cut

3 tbsp extra virgin olive oil

1 tbsp paprika

½ tsp black pepper

1 tsp salt

Directions:

Heat olive oil in an ovenproof casserole dish and gently sauté the chopped onions for 1-2 minutes. Stir in paprika and rice and cook, stirring constantly for another minute.

Add in beans and a cup of water or vegetable broth, season with salt and black pepper, stir in mint and parsley and bake in a preheated to 350 F oven for 20 minutes.

Italian Eggplant Parmesan

Serves: 6

Prep time: 1 hr 10 min

Ingredients:

2 large eggplants, sliced

3 cups tomato sauce

2 cups mozzarella cheese, shredded

½ cup Parmesan cheese, grated

3 tbsp olive oil

1 tsp basil

salt and black pepper, to taste

Directions:

Fry eggplant slices in olive oil until soft.

Layer eggplant, tomato sauce, mozzarella, and Parmesan in casserole dish. Repeat layers.

Top with remaining cheese and basil. Bake at 375F for 40 minutes until golden.

Green Pea and Rice Casserole

Serves: 4-5

Prep time: 20 min

Ingredients:

1 onion, chopped

1 1 lb bag frozen peas

3 garlic cloves, chopped

3-4 mushrooms, chopped

2/3 cup white rice

1 cup water

2/3 cup grated Parmezan cheese

4 tbsp extra virgin olive oil

salt and black pepper, to taste

Directions:

In a deep ovenproof casserole dish, heat olive oil and sauté the onions, garlic and mushrooms for 2-3 minutes. Add in the rice and cook, stirring constantly for 1 minute.

Add in a cup of warm water and the frozen peas, stir and bake in a preheated to 350 F oven for 20 minutes.

Sprinkle with Parmesan cheese, bake for 2-3 more minutes and serve.

Ratatouille

Serves: 4

Prep time: 45 min

Ingredients:

1 eggplant, peeled and diced

2 large tomatoes, diced

2 zucchinis, peeled and sliced

1 onion, sliced

1 green pepper, sliced

6-7 mushrooms, sliced

3 cloves garlic, crushed

1 tbsp dried parsley

3 tbsp extra virgin olive oil

salt, to taste

Directions:

Place eggplant on a tray and sprinkle it with salt. Set aside for 30 minutes, then rinse and pat dry.

Heat olive oil in an ovenproof casserole dish over medium heat. Gently sauté garlic until fragrant.

Add in parsley and eggplant and cook until eggplant is soft. Spread zucchinis in an even layer over the eggplant. Layer onion, mushrooms, pepper and tomatoes, and bake in a preheated to 350 F oven for 40 minutes.

Easy Okra and Tomato Casserole

Serves: 4

Prep time: 25 min

Ingredients:

1 lb okra, trimmed

3 tomatoes, cut into wedges

3 garlic cloves, chopped

1 cup fresh parsley leaves, finely cut

3 tbsp extra virgin olive oil

1 tsp salt

black pepper, to taste

Directions:

In a deep ovenproof baking dish, combine okra, sliced tomatoes, olive oil and garlic.

Add in salt and black pepper to taste, and toss to combine.

Bake in a preheated to 350 F oven for 45 minutes, or until the okra is tender.

Sprinkle with parsley and serve.

Potato and Zucchini Casserole

Serves: 5-6

Prep time: 25 min

Ingredients:

1 lb potatoes, peeled and sliced

4-5 zucchinis, peeled and sliced

1 onion, sliced

2 garlic cloves, crushed

½ cup water

4 tbsp extra virgin olive oil

1 tsp dry oregano

1/3 cup fresh dill, chopped

salt and black pepper, to taste

Directions:

Place the potatoes, zucchinis and onion in a shallow ovenproof baking dish. Pour over the olive oil and water. Add salt, black pepper to taste, and toss everything together.

Bake in a preheated to 350 F oven for 40 minutes, stirring halfway through, bake for 5 minutes more and serve.

Cauliflower Casserole

Serves 6

Prep time: 35 min

Ingredients:

1 head cauliflower, cut in small florets

1 large red pepper, chopped

1 onion, finely chopped

4 garlic cloves, chopped

1 tsp dried thyme

2 tbsp extra virgin olive oil

8 oz shredded cheddar cheese, divided

8 oz shredded Monterey Jack cheese, divided

1 cup sour cream

salt and black pepper, to taste

Directions:

Steam cauliflower florets until tender, about 8 minutes.

Heat olive oil in a large skillet and sauté onion, garlic and the red pepper until fragrant. Stir in thyme.

Stir cauliflower and onion mixture together in an ovenproof casserole. Season with salt and pepper to taste.

Combine sour cream, 6 oz of the shredded cheddar and 6 oz of the Monterey Jack and stir it in the casserole. Sprinkle on top remaining cheddar and Monterey Jack cheese.

Cover the casserole with foil and bake for 25 minute, remove foil and bake until cheese is brown and bubbly.

Hearty Quinoa and Spinach Breakfast Casserole

Serves: 4

Prep time: 30 min

Ingredients:

1 cup cooked quinoa

3-4 spring onions, finely chopped

5 oz frozen chopped spinach, thawed and squeezed dry

½ zucchini, peeled and shredded

5 eggs

1/2 cup milk

4 tbsp extra virgin olive oil

salt and black pepper, to taste

1 cup cheddar cheese, grated

Directions:

In a large bowl combine eggs, milk, salt and pepper.

In a deep casserole dish heat the olive oil. Cook the onions, zucchini and spinach, stirring constantly, until lightly cooked. Add in the quinoa and combine everything well. Pour the egg mixture over and then top with cheddar cheese.

Bake in a preheated to 350 F oven for 20 minutes.

Baked Shakshuka Casserole

Serves: 4

Prep time: 35 min

Ingredients:

4 eggs

1 onion, chopped

2 bell peppers, sliced

3 cups tomato sauce

2 tbsp olive oil

1 tsp cumin

1 tsp paprika

salt and black pepper, to taste

½ cup fresh parsley, finely cut

Directions:

Sauté onion and peppers in olive oil.

Add tomato sauce, cumin, paprika, salt, and black pepper. Simmer for 10 minutes.

Transfer to casserole dish, make wells, and crack eggs into them. Bake at 375F for 10-12 minutes or until eggs are set. Serve sprinkled with parsley.

Greek Zucchini and Cheese Casserole

Serves: 4

Prep time: 50 min

Ingredients:

3 zucchini, grated

1 onion, chopped

4 eggs, whisked

1 cup feta cheese, crumbled

3 tbsp olive oil

1 tbsp dill

salt and black pepper, to taste

Directions:

In a skillet, sauté zucchini and onion in olive oil.

Cool slightly, then mix with eggs, feta, dill, salt, and black pepper.

Pour into a casserole dish. Bake at 375F for 35 minutes until set and golden.

Spanish Potato Casserole

Serves: 4

Prep time: 45 min

Ingredients:

4 potatoes, peeled and sliced

2 onions, sliced

2 bell peppers, sliced

3 tbsp olive oil

1 tsp paprika

salt and black pepper, to taste

Directions:

Layer potatoes, onions, and peppers in a casserole dish.

Drizzle with olive oil and sprinkle with paprika, salt, and black pepper.

Cover and bake at 375F for 35 minutes. Remove cover and bake 10 minutes more until crisp.

Greek Breakfast Casserole

Serves: 6

Prep time: 45-50 minutes

Ingredients:

8 large eggs

5 cups baby spinach

1 onion, diced

2 cloves garlic, minced

1 cup milk

1/2 tsp dried dill

2 tbsp extra-virgin olive oil

1/4 tsp red pepper flakes

salt and black pepper, to taste

1/2 cup chopped kalamata olives

1/2 cup crumbled feta cheese

1/2 cup sun-dried tomatoes, chopped

1/3 cup grated Parmesan cheese

Directions:

Preheat the oven to 375F.

Heat olive oil in a large skillet over medium heat. Add onion and cook for 5 minutes until softened. Add in garlic and cook for 30 seconds more.

Add the spinach and cook until wilted, about 2 minutes. Remove from heat set aside to cool slightly.

In a mixing bowl, whisk together eggs, milk, dill, red pepper, salt, and black pepper. Stir in the spinach mixture, olives, feta, and sun-dried tomatoes.

Pour into a greased casserole dish and sprinkle Parmesan over the top. Bake for about 40 minutes, or until the center is set and golden.

Cool for 5 minutes, slice and serve warm with a drizzle of olive oil.

Mediterranean Vegetable Breakfast Casserole

Serves: 6

Prep time: 45 minutes

Ingredients:

1 small red onion, finely chopped

1 red bell pepper, diced

1 small zucchini, peeled and diced

1 cup cherry tomatoes, halved

2 cups baby spinach, chopped

8 large eggs

2 tbsp extra virgin olive oil

1/2 cup milk

1 tsp dried oregano

Salt and black pepper, to taste

1/3 cup crumbled feta cheese

2 tbsp chopped fresh basil or parsley

Directions:

Preheat the oven to 375F.

Heat olive oil in a skillet over medium heat and gently sauté onion, bell pepper, and zucchini. Cook for 5-6 minutes until softened. Add in spinach and tomatoes and cook for 2 minutes more.

In a large bowl, whisk the eggs, milk, oregano, salt, and pepper. Stir in the sautéed vegetables and feta cheese.

Pour the mixture into a greased casserole dish. Bake for 35-40 minutes, or until the eggs are set and the top is golden.

Set aside to cool slightly, sprinkle with fresh herbs, and serve warm or at room temperature.

Bonus: Delicious Low Fat Soup Recipes Inspired by the Mediterranean Diet

Mediterranean Chicken Soup

Serves: 6-8

Prep time: 35 min

Ingredients:

3 chicken breast halves

2 carrots, chopped

1 celery stalk, chopped

1/2 onion, chopped

1/3 cup rice

8 cups water

1/2 cup black olives, pitted and halved

salt and black pepper, to taste

1/2 cup fresh coriander, finely cut, to serve

lemon juice, to serve

Directions:

Place chicken breasts in a soup pot together with onion, carrots, celery, salt, black pepper, and water.

Bring to a boil, add in rice and olives, stir, and reduce heat.

Simmer for 30-35 minutes then remove the chicken from the pot and let it cool slightly.

Shred the chicken and return it back to the pot. Stir, and serve sprinkled with fresh coriander and lemon juice.

Greek Chicken Soup

Serves: 4-5

Prep time: 35 min

Ingredients:

3 chicken breast halves, diced

1/3 cup rice

4 cups chicken broth

1 small onion, finely cut

3 raw egg yolks

1/2 cup fresh lemon juice

3 tbsp extra virgin olive oil

1 tsp salt

1/2 tsp black pepper

1/2 cup fresh parsley, finely cut, to serve

Directions:

In a soup pot, heat the olive oil and gently sauté the onion until translucent. Add in the chicken broth and bring to a boil.

Stir in the rice and the chicken, reduce heat, and simmer until the rice is almost done.

Whisk the egg yolks and lemon juice together in a small bowl. Gently add in a cup of the chicken soup whisking constantly. Return this mixture to the chicken soup and stir well to blend. Do not boil any more.

Season with salt and pepper and garnish with finely chopped parsley. Serve hot.

Fish and Noodle Soup

Serves: 6-7

Prep time: 15 min

Ingredients:

4 white fish fillets, cut into strips

2 carrots, cut into ribbons

1 zucchini, peeled and cut into ribbons

5-6 white button mushrooms, sliced

1 celery stalk, finely cut

1 cup baby spinach

7 oz rice noodles

3 cups vegetable broth

2 cups water

3 tbsp soy sauce

1 tsp ground ginger

salt and black pepper, to taste

Directions:

Place vegetable broth, water and soy sauce in a deep soup pot. Bring to a boil and add carrots, celery, zucchini, mushrooms and ginger.

Simmer, partially covered, for 5 minutes then add in the fish and noodles and simmer for 5 minutes more or until the fish is cooked through.

Stir in baby spinach and cook until it wilts. Season with black pepper and salt to taste and serve.

Lamb Soup

Serves 4-5

Prep time: 45-50 min

Ingredients:

2 lbs lean boneless lamb, cubed

1 onion, finely cut

1 carrot, chopped

10-15 spring onions, chopped

4 cups water

2 tbsp extra virgin olive oil

1/2 tsp paprika

black pepper, to taste

1/2 cup fresh mint, finely cut

1/2 cup fresh parsley, finely cut

2 eggs

Directions:

In a deep soup pot, heat olive oil and gently brown the lamb cubes. Add in the onion and carrot and sauté for 2-3 minutes, stirring. Add in paprika and water. Bring to the boil, then lower heat to medium-low and simmer until the lamb softens.

Add spring onions, mint, parsley, salt and black pepper. Bring to a boil again and simmer for 5 minutes.

Whisk the eggs in a small bowl. Take one ladle from the soup and add into the egg mixture. Stir to combine. Take another ladle and stir again. Pour the egg back into into the soup and stir. Do not boil again. Serve hot.

Creamy Potato Soup

Serves: 4-5

Prep time: 35 min

Ingredients:

6 medium potatoes, cut into small cubes

1 leek, white part only, chopped

1 carrot, chopped

1 zucchini, peeled and chopped

1 celery stalk, chopped

3 cups water

1 cup milk

3 tbsp extra virgin olive oil

salt and black pepper, to taste

Directions:

Gently heat olive oil in a deep saucepan and sauté the onion for 2-3 minutes. Add in potatoes, carrot, zucchini and celery and cook for 2-3 minutes, stirring.

Add in water and salt and bring to a boil, then lower heat and simmer until the vegetables are tender. Blend until smooth, add milk, blend some more and serve.

Leek, Brown Rice and Potato Soup

Serves: 4-5

Prep time: 35 min

Ingredients:

3 potatoes, peeled and diced

2 leeks, finely chopped

1/4 cup brown rice

5 cups water

3 tbsp extra virgin olive oil

lemon juice, to taste

Directions:

Heat olive oil in a deep soup pot and sauté leeks for 3-4 minutes. Add in potatoes and cook for a minute more.

Stir in water, bring to a boil, and the brown rice. Reduce heat and simmer for 30 minutes. Add lemon juice, to taste, and serve.

Fast Mediterranean Chickpea Soup

Serves: 5-6

Prep time: 30 min

Ingredients:

1 can (15 oz) chickpeas, drained

1 small onion, chopped

2 garlic cloves, minced

1 can (15 oz) tomatoes, diced

2 cups vegetable broth

1 cup milk

3 tbsp extra virgin olive oil

2 bay leaves

1/2 tsp dried oregano

Directions:

Heat olive oil in a deep soup pot and sauté onion and garlic for 1-2 minutes. Add in broth, chickpeas, tomatoes, bay leaves, and oregano.

Bring the soup to a boil then reduce heat and simmer for 20 minutes. Add in milk and cook for 1-2 minutes more. Set aside to cool, discard the bay leaves and blend until smooth.

About the Author

Alissa Grey is a fitness and nutrition enthusiast who loves to teach people about losing weight and feeling better about themselves. She lives in a small French village in the foothills of a beautiful mountain range with her husband, three teenage kids, two free spirited dogs, and various other animals.

Alissa is incredibly lucky to be able to cook and eat natural foods, mostly grown nearby, something she's done since she was a teenager. She enjoys yoga, running, reading, hanging out with her family, and growing organic vegetables and herbs.

Printed in Dunstable, United Kingdom